What lies behind us
and what lies before us
are small matters
compared to what lies within us.

— Ralph Waldo Emerson

The Smallest things

make the biggest difference.®

Change your thoughts · Change your world

Ray Haring, Ph.D.

HealthSpan ®
COMMUNICATIONS

Acknowledgments

To my family, friends, and those who understand
that joy, love, and peace are life's greatest treasures.

My sincerest appreciation and special thanks are extended to
Gay Carroll and Jackie Boor for their editorial assistance.

Graphic design: Ellen Baxter in association
with HealthSpan Communications®

Cartoons: John Kloss in association with
HealthSpan Communications®

HealthSpan Communications,
the HealthSpan Communications logo, and
The Smallest Things Make the Biggest Difference,
are all registered trademarks
of HealthSpan Communications.

First Edition, 1999

Library of Congress Catalog Card Number 97-04621

ISBN 0-9643673-2-7
UPC 69086101295500002

www.smallestthings.com
email: healthspan@smallestthings.com

Publisher's Note

This book is solely intended for educational purposes and is not meant whatsoever to serve as a substitute for medical, therapeutic, or any other professional advice or counsel. Assistance involving any aspect of personal health should be addressed by a licensed physician or certified professional in the field.

PRINTED IN THE UNITED STATES OF AMERICA

There is little difference in people,
but that little difference makes a big difference.
The little difference is attitude.
The big difference is whether it is positive or negative.

— Clement Stone

Introduction

This book celebrates the miracle of how the smallest things can make the biggest differences in our physical, emotional, and spiritual well-being.

As you explore the thoughts and messages expressed in the pages to come, you will be touched, inspired, and enlightened.

It is my hope that you come to appreciate that the smallest things that you see or don't see—believe or don't believe—do or don't do—will make the biggest difference in the direction of your life.

To your health.
Best always,

Raymond V. Haring, Ph.D.
President, HealthSpan Communications®

Contents

Contents

Contents

Contents

Contents

Doors to extraordinary places can be opened
if you have the right keys.

Little Keys Open Big Doors

C hildren are fascinated by keys. They learn early how keys can open locked doors and start cars. For me, keys came with my first bicycle, toy treasure chest, and piggy bank. Misplacing a key meant losing access to my belongings. Remember how frustrating it was shaking those banks and hoping the coins would somehow tumble out?

As adults, we have even more to lose or be denied if we're missing important *keys*. While we can quickly replace keys to our doors and cars, keys to the future are not so easily made. These are the little keys that unlock big doors and allow us to live our dreams. They are nothing more than simple values that we learn and use every day. These keys will never be lost if we learn and remember where they are and how to use them.

Doors to extraordinary places can be opened with even the smallest keys. Since this book deals with unlocking doors, I'll tell you about the simplest key ever known to unlock and tap into the world's largest piggy bank.

The key is very simple: Enrich another's life and you will be rewarded. The size of these rewards will mirror the value we bring to other lives.

Andrew Carnegie, the richest man of his time, spoke to this truth when he said, "No man can become rich without himself enriching others."

When we're helping others, we're essentially helping ourselves. So grab your keys and open a *door* for someone today.

Touch with Your Heart—Not with Your Hands

*The best and most beautiful things
in the world cannot be seen or even touched.
They must be felt with the heart.*

— Elbert Hubbard

Small Gifts Are Never Forgotten

The wrapping paper had lost its sheen long ago and the elegant bow and ribbons had not been seen in as many years. But the gift his daughter gave him two decades ago remains under his bed to this day.

For years, he had thought his duty as a father was to provide food, clothing, and a roof for his children. Sometimes, this meant working two full-time jobs and, even then, his family was barely able to make ends meet. Special times were few and far between, so on his birthday, when his 12-year-old daughter handed him a large, exquisitely wrapped present, the swell of anticipation momentarily washed away all the worries.

The wrapping paper was beautiful and topped with a shiny bow bigger than his fist.

"Go on, Daddy," his daughter urged eagerly, "open it."

He hurriedly unwrapped the gift and lifted the lid, only to find the box empty. "What kind of sense does this make?" he asked. "There is nothing here but fancy paper and a big bow."

His daughter's fragile smile disappeared. "I didn't have very much time or money . . ."

He pressed, "So you spent it this way? Wrapping an empty box? That's rather foolish, isn't it?"

"It isn't empty," she meekly offered.

He turned the box upside down and shook it. Nothing came out. "Sure seems empty to me."

"Before . . ." she paused, with a look on her face that he would hold in his memory forever . . . "before I wrapped it, I blew a kiss into the box."

In an instant, the box grew heavy in his hands, and he saw inside much more than a kiss.

He saw a beautiful daughter.

Priceless as a Smile

Much happiness is overlooked
simply because it doesn't cost anything.

— Prism

If You Want to Keep It—Give It Away

There are a few things in life that we can never lose as long as we remember to give them away each day.

Love.

Kindness.

And understanding.

These are just a few of the things that we must give to others if we wish to keep them for ourselves.

This idea is beautifully illustrated with a thought by Antonio Porchia. "In a full heart there is room for everything, and in an empty heart there is room for nothing."

Our hearts become full when we share with others the things we hold inside.

Blessed are those that can give
without remembering
and take without forgetting.

— Elizabeth Bibesco

Love Beyond First Sight

Love at first sight is easy to understand;
it's when two people have been looking at each
other for a lifetime that it becomes a miracle.

— Sam Levenson

We're All Composers

One of my pastimes is listening to beautiful music. We all have favorite singers and musicians who have written and performed melodies that touch us in some special way.

But there's one thing even sweeter than our favorite music. Soft words of praise, encouragement, recognition, and appreciation are always music to our ears.

"The sweetest of all sounds," according to Greek historian Xenophon, "is praise."

Try your hand at *songwriting* by composing a few bars of praise and *performing* for someone you love. You may even get a standing ovation, and the appreciation you receive will make you want to compose more melodies.

The Art of Making Friends

The only way to have a friend
is to be a friend.

— Ralph Waldo Emerson

Build a Miracle Piece by Piece

Do you remember the day astronauts Neil Armstrong and Buzz Aldrin landed on the surface of the moon? It was July 20, 1969.

The attention of the entire world was focused on a few tiny steps taken on the lunar surface.

"One small step for man, one giant leap for mankind" was transmitted back to Earth in seconds as radio transmission waves raced two hundred thousand miles across empty space toward Earth.

Was the landing a miracle?

Some people believe it was. But for the crew, engineers, scientists, and all the thousands of other people devoted to this mission, the lunar landing was a mind-boggling project, orchestrated by billions of creative thoughts and assembled with sufficient perfection to guarantee not only a safe lunar landing, but a welcome return to Earth. After counting the millions of hours that went into preflight details, the success of the lunar landing was really a task attributable to hard work and dedication, rather than a miracle.

Although most of us will probably never have the chance to travel in space, we will all have the opportunity to piece together miracles every day in our own lives, right here on Earth.

Leonard Nimoy, the man who traveled billions of miles as Mr. Spock *Star Trekking* across television screens on the fictional Starship Enterprise, knew that the real miracle is this: "The more we share, the more we have."

Each time we share a moment of laughter, an instant of empathy, or a piece of trust, we're given far more than what we started with—we're given a miraculous feeling called happiness.

And this happiness, or *miracle,* can be enjoyed right here on Earth, without having to travel to far-away places.

Turn up the lights and raise the curtains —
you're on stage!

A Life Performance

If you're looking for an answer to "what makes me, me?," consider the brief but lasting thoughts of a former pupil of Plato. In just six words, the Greek philosopher Aristotle, two millennia ago, explained, "We are what we repeatedly do."

Sounds reasonable.

But finding a way to define *life* is a bit more involved. For starters, consider what Roman emperor and philosopher Marcus Aurelius offered. "Your life," he wrote, "is an expression of all your thoughts."

Makes perfect sense.

So what are we to do?

Be careful what you do *and* what you think about. Life is always in the "forward play" mode; it can't be stopped, rewound, or replayed—it's always playing.

Whatever you put in your mind, and whatever you repeatedly do, all go to make you who you are.

"Life isn't a dress rehearsal," as the famous saying goes. "It's the real thing."

Enjoy a *life* performance like no other.

Turn up the lights and raise the curtains—you're *always* on stage!

Man is born to live and not to prepare to live.

— Boris Pasternak

Stop Looking for Happiness

One of the surest ways to find happiness for yourself is to devote your energies toward making someone else happy. Happiness is an elusive, transitory thing. And if you set out to search for it, you will find it evasive. But if you try to bring happiness to someone else, then it comes to you.

— Napoleon Hill

A Glass Half Empty Is Still Half Full

Occasionally, it's a good idea to think about one of life's most basic truths.

A glass that is half empty is still half full.

Whether we call this phenomenon hope or optimism, the result is the same—a winning, unstoppable attitude.

Can you think of one good reason for being a pessimist?

Sir Winston Churchill couldn't when he wrote, "I am an optimist. It does not seem too much use being anything else."

There are countless reasons for being positive. The most obvious is that we're stuck with ourselves, so we might as well enjoy the ride!

Next time you're wondering if your life is half full or half empty, you'll know what to do—fill it up! This way, you won't have to wonder if your glass is half empty or half full.

Get busy!

Find a fire hose and start filling your glass to the brim. Imagine the joy when it overflows!

Give and You Will Receive

No person was ever honored for what he received.
Honor has been the reward for what he gave.

— Calvin Coolidge

Small Acts of Kindness

M oney and loans usually come from banks. *Gifts* come from our hearts and have no repayment plan.

The most treasured gifts are acts of kindness or simple words that touch our souls when whispered into our ears.

"Kind words," said Mother Teresa, "can be short and easy to speak, but their echoes are truly endless."

Long ago, William Penn, the English Quaker and founder of Pennsylvania, offered a gift of wisdom that echoes through time, when he wrote, "I expect to pass through this world but once. Any good therefore that I can do, or any kindness or abilities that I can show to any fellow creature, let me do it now. Let me not defer or neglect it, for I shall not pass this way again."

What small act of kindness can you accomplish today?

The only gift is a portion of thyself.

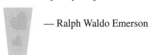

— Ralph Waldo Emerson

Be Flexible with Your Age

If wrinkles must be written upon our brows,
let them not be written upon the heart.
The spirit should not grow old.

— James A. Garfield

Ageless Advice

No one wants to get old, but no one wants a short life, either.

So how can we find a balance between the inevitable and our desire for a long life?

For starters, toss the notion that aging means getting old, acting old, or giving up on youthful dreams. According to John Noe, "A person doesn't become old until his regrets take the place of his dreams."

As the years go by, we discover that *age* has more to do with our spirit than it does with the number of candles placed on a birthday cake.

A young women of 80 years once said, "One should never count the years, one should instead count one's interests. I have kept young trying never to lose my childhood sense of wonderment." Her name was Helen Keller, and her ageless spirit allowed her to remain youthful and achieve greatness despite the deafness and blindness she developed as a child.

In the view of Dr. Norman Cousins, "Death is not the greatest loss in life. The greatest loss is what dies inside us while we live."

So, grab life by the horns!

Forget about the number of candles on your last birthday cake. One large sparkler boldly standing in the middle of the cake will make its own statement about age and allow ample time to make as many wishes as you want.

To be able to look back upon one's life
with satisfaction is to live twice.

— Martial

No Age Limit

Love is only for the young,
the middle aged, and the old.

— Anonymous

You're as Young as You Think You Are

How old do you feel?
How old do you act?

These are entirely different questions, and depending on whom you ask, you will frequently get different answers.

Some people think life is too short, while others think life is much too long—especially if stranded in a traffic jam or waiting for someone who happens to be running late. Albert Einstein was right, time *is* relative.

Leonardo da Vinci wrote, "Life well spent is long."

Doing activities that keep our bodies active and strong, and our minds alert and curious, brings out the youthfulness of our smiles and the beauty of our souls. There are people who are sedentary and old at 20, and then there are others who are young and active at 60, 70, and 80 years of age.

Age really is a state of mind and body.

Consider the *age* of a man who celebrated one of his birthdays towing 70 boats for one mile across Long Beach Harbor. He was 70 years young at the time of this feat. Jack LaLanne never let his age conquer his spirit and desire to remain young.

Michelangelo, the famous Italian poet, sculptor, architect, and painter who lived from 1475 to 1564, produced some of his best work when he was in his seventies. His completion of the magnificent frescos in the Sistene Chapel is a testament and reminder to anyone that age is indeed in the eyes of the beholder.

Some people refuse to ever get *old*.

"Retirement at 65 is ridiculous. When I was 65, I still had pimples," said comedian George Burns, who remained youthful until he left us at 100 years of age.

So, think young and live long.

To your youth!

Walls that Leave Us Unprotected

Generally, walls and fences are built to protect people from losing things they value. We assume the thicker the wall or higher the fence, the greater our safety.

This practice, however, is why so many of life's treasures not only escape our grasp, but are left unshared. In our desire to protect ourselves, we can actually deprive ourselves of wonderful opportunities to learn, grow, and love.

In short, we sacrifice or sabotage our interests by trying to hold on to them too tightly.

When we build walls, relationships and friendships become strained, and communication, trust, and intimacy eventually collapse under the weight of these walls.

Joseph Newton sums it up best. "People are lonely because they build walls instead of bridges."

Sad, but true.

Whether we're gregarious or reclusive, there is one thing for certain—we will always be able to hold more in our hearts and carry more in our arms than with closed minds and clenched fists.

Protect yourself.

Open your heart to those who love you.

Unspoken Words Speak the Loudest

Sometimes—Role modeling is unconscious!

The most basic research reveals that people do as they see, not as they are told. By setting examples and not by issuing commands, we have impact and best inspire others to be their best.

Many famous and not-so-famous people have shaped the thoughts and actions of others without ever speaking a single word to them.

Albert Einstein once said, "Setting an example is not the main means of influencing another, it is the only means."

We Learn by Opening Our Minds—Not Our Mouths

One of the first things I learned in life was that much more could be learned with my ears and eyes than with my mouth.

Our vocal cords were not designed for learning. They were designed to allow us to share with others what we've already learned with our own eyes and ears.

A few thousand years ago, Socrates wrote, "There is only one good, knowledge, and one evil, ignorance."

I think Socrates understood why people have twice as many ears and twice as many eyes as they have mouths. Wisdom isn't learned by opening our mouths—it's gained by opening our minds.

"Wisdom," according to Doug Larson, "is the reward you get for a lifetime of listening when you'd have preferred to talk."

Now, I'll be quiet.

First Understand—Then Be Understood

*Communication does not begin with being understood,
but with understanding others.*

— W. Steven Brown

I Know What I Said—
But That's Not What I Meant

To a team of mountain climbers, life and death hinge on hearing the subtle difference between the words "let's go" and "let go."

Clarity of speech and clarity of hearing are equally important when we communicate.

In less serious situations, sometimes one word or just one letter makes the difference between a compliment and a complaint, or the difference between success and failure. Removing the letter "t" from "I can't" increases our chances of succeeding a thousandfold.

Mark Twain became famous by carefully choosing words *and* letters to tell stories. He knew exactly what he meant when he said, "A powerful agent is the right word."

Of the 600,000 words in the English language from which we can choose, most of us use only a few thousand to communicate our thoughts. It's no wonder that library shelves are lined with books on how to improve communication skills.

"I know you believe you understand what you think I said, but I am not sure you realize that what you heard is not what I meant," wrote an anonymous author.

Adding just a few new words to your repertoire each week can build an astounding vocabulary that will make the difference between saying something you didn't intend to say and saying something you actually meant.

The Two Most Appreciated Words

" Thank you."
These two words convey so much when spoken or written–
yet, may say even more when they're not.

Use them often and freely.

You will always have a captive audience wanting to
hear more. For special effects, add a smile, a handshake, or
an embrace.

Speak kind words and you will hear kind echoes.

 — Bahn

You Said Everything by Saying Nothing

The *little* things we don't say or do can be as important as what we actually say or do.

How often have you meant to communicate something other than what you said?

Too often, I suspect!

There are also times when saying nothing or doing nothing communicates the wrong message. For instance, remaining silent when a response was not only appropriate, but necessary.

Other times, we beautifully communicate without using a single word. Consider the message delivered by a warm hand extended to a person in need of friendship or comfort.

Dorothy Nevill had her finger on the point when she explained, "The art of communication is not only to say the right thing at the right place, but to leave unsaid the wrong thing at the tempting moment."

And then again, so much of what is communicated has never been spoken. "The most important thing in communication," Peter Drucker once said, "is to hear what isn't being said."

Listen carefully to the *sounds* emanating from silence.

With practice, you'll hear subtleties and nuances in communication without hearing a single word spoken.

Expand Your Horizons

I know of no more encouraging fact
than the unquestionable ability of man
to elevate his life by a conscious endeavor.

— Henry David Thoreau

Rooms Without Walls

One of the thinnest and most difficult lines to see is the line we draw between self-acceptance and the desire for self-improvement.

Striving toward excellence is a desirable trait as well as a wonderful goal. Accepting little imperfections in ourselves, however, is healthy.

"Maturity is the ability to live in peace with that which we cannot change." Thank you, Ann Landers.

There isn't anyone who doesn't want to make some kind of personal adjustment. This desire to make improvements doesn't mean we're unhappy or flawed. It simply means we're evolving, creating new facets, and exploring new spaces in our lives. And we're doing this in a *room* without windows, doors, or even walls.

The room is as spacious or cluttered as we choose.

Sometimes we have company.

Other times we're alone.

Always, we have options.

Yes, the largest room in the world is the room for self-improvement.

Visits are strongly encouraged.

There are no set visiting hours.

Stay as long as you like.

Endless Opportunities

The unexamined life is not worth living.

— Socrates

Groundhog Days

Once upon a time, there was a little groundhog who worked tirelessly day in and day out, year after year. His accomplishments were evident by the large number of holes and lengthy tunnels he dug in the ground.

One day a group of surveyors happened upon the groundhog while he was busy at work. Puzzled by the feverish pace and long hours that the groundhog spent working each day, the surveyors asked the groundhog why he was digging so many holes. The groundhog simply replied that he hadn't given it much thought. He felt the frantic pace of his life did not allow him the time to consider such ridiculous questions.

Have you ever felt like a groundhog, so busy working that you simply didn't have the time to look up and evaluate the path you're blazing?

A lot of work gets done on *Groundhog Days*, but not necessarily the work that really needs to get done. It's analogous to walking in place—you're tired at the end of the day, but you haven't gotten anywhere.

There are some folks who schedule so many *Groundhog Days* on their calendar that they're actually living *Groundhog Lives*.

It's easy to identify people living *Groundhog Lives*.

They hurry.

And they scurry.

And they do it without knowing where, why, or what they're doing.

There are, however, a few remedies for their symptoms.

Self-reflection.

Brief moments of pause.

And a little relaxation.

Build a Career Without Working

It may not come as a surprise to you that a huge segment of America's work force dislikes or is dissatisfied with their jobs. The actual percentage of dissatisfied workers is not particularly important. What is important is to realize that very few people ever become successful, let alone happy, when they continue in a job or a career they find unfulfilling.

An essential ingredient to successful and fulfilling work is finding enjoyment and pleasure in what you do. Consider the career of a man who failed thousands of times, who worked tirelessly for long years throughout his life, who said, "I never did a day's work in my life. It was all fun." This man was Thomas Edison.

It's not necessary that we thumb through history books looking for famous workaholics who discovered that working could be a way of blissfully spending their time in a productive manner. Rather, we must continue to search for new ways to view or find work that offers an opportunity to enjoy the eight hours a day most of us spend working.

Here's a formula for success.

Think about just one thing for which you have tremendous passion that will also in some way provide a valuable product or service to others. Then build your enthusiasm until you are willing to take whatever steps are necessary to make your vision a reality.

This simple equation for success has led many people to choose careers that are both rewarding and fulfilling.

Tired of Working?

S ome people don't like to work, but unfortunately, bills need to get paid and certain things just need to get done.

Consequently, with this dilemma in mind, we head off to another day of work. Has the grind ever gotten to the point where you have thought about making a career change to avoid *working*?

If you're dissatisfied with your work, or just plain tired of working, then consider the advice of Confucius, a Chinese philosopher who lived 2,500 years ago. "Choose a job you love, and you will never have to work a day in your life."

Too simple?

Comedian George Burns knew this secret when he said, "Fall in love with what you are going to do for a living. To be able to get out of bed and do what you love to do for the rest of the day is beyond words. I'd rather be a failure in something that I love than be successful in something that I hate."

It's old thinking that work can't be fun, exciting and lucrative—all at the same time.

Why Work So Hard? Half Days Will Do Just Fine

Why work so hard?

It seems there is far greater potential to tire and make mistakes the longer and harder we work. It's a very well known physiological fact that routine rests and naps, besides the traditional eight hours of sleep, are necessary to rejuvenate the mind, body, and soul.

Could the old work ethic of working long, full days to get ahead be outdated?

Kemmons Wilson, founder of Holiday Inn, failed to do the work necessary to receive his high school diploma. Yet, because of his phenomenal business success, Mr. Wilson was asked at a much later date to deliver a commencement speech for one of the school's graduating classes. He made a simple point by saying, "I really don't know why I'm here. I never got a degree and I've only worked half days my entire life. My advice to you is to do the same. Work half days every day. It does not matter which half you work—the first 12 hours or the second 12 hours."

Similar thoughts were echoed by J.C. Penney, founder of one of the largest retail stores in the country, who said, "Give me a stock clerk who wants to work and I will give you a person who will make history. Give me a person who does not want to work, and I will give you a stock clerk."

One of the best messages about working long or short hours comes from the famous architect Frank Lloyd Wright. "A professional," he said, "is one who does his best work when he feels the least like working."

If we seek work that brings a sense of fulfillment, satisfaction, or, better yet, joy, then we won't think twice about working one of Mr. Wilson's 12-hour days.

The Beginning of a Journey

S omething very interesting is unfolding in this picture.
People are predicting what will eventually become their

reality, simply because they're subscribing to certain beliefs.

It's called a self-fulfilling prophecy and it works like this: A belief about something causes us to act accordingly.

Picture yourself as the creator of a self-fulfilling prophecy. For instance, you may initially believe you can't do something; therefore, you don't try.

Without trying, nothing happens.

When *nothing* happens, you have proof that your self-fulfilling prophecy was accurate.

A self-fulfilling prophecy doesn't have to be negative or self-defeating; it can be constructive if used in a positive way. All of us have made predictions based on past experiences and beliefs. The trick is learning to make self-fulfilling prophecies that are positive or health-supporting rather than limiting or self-defeating.

Your potential is reached by *believing* in your abilities. What you see as being possible, what you believe as being likely, and what you value as being sacred, will be who you become.

The continuation of your journey begins with your next self-fulfilling prophecy.

What will it be?

A Road Map for All Occasions

Have you ever tallied the number of decisions you face in a single day?

Hundreds, perhaps!

It's no mystery that certain decisions are effortless to make, while others require tons of thought. Indecision keeps many of us going back and forth and makes us feel uncertain about where we're headed or what we're trying to do.

Do these thoughts sound familiar?

"I don't know what to do or where to go."

"I'm lost."

If so, you may want to read a map.

One of my favorites is a *one-way* road map. If you ever get lost using this map, just remember to always go forward. You never turn back.

The famous explorer David Livingstone understood the power of this one-way map when he wrote, "I will go anywhere, as long as it is forward."

Part of being able to use this one-way road map is to understand that when you make a decision to go forward, your values are driving your decisions. These values are principles you hold in very high regard and which act as a guidance system inside you.

The next time you're faced with indecision, simply draw on your values, get out your road map, consider the issue, make a decision, and don't look back!

After you've used the road map for a while, you'll get used to how easy it is.

Good luck and happy traveling.

First Things First

Nothing happens unless first a dream.

— Carl Sandburg

Aiming at Nothing and Hitting It Every Time

I was about eight or nine years old when I got my first bow and arrow set.

I never had a set of paper targets because all of my arrows were fitted with rubber suction tips. Any arrow that would have been shot at a paper target would have simply fallen or bounced off. So instead, I had plenty of fun firing the arrows into the sky. Eventually, I lost all of my arrows without ever improving my aim or score.

How many times have you *aimed* without a target or goal in mind?

More than once?

If we had an endless supply of arrows and time, we could afford to pay less attention to the direction and focus of our thoughts and goals.

There is, however, a way to hit a bull's-eye every time without ever having to take aim. Simply pull an arrow from your quiver and, without any thought given to its destination, fire the arrow high into the sky. Take cover. When it finally strikes the ground, it will have hit the *target*. Now draw a small circle around the point of impact. Bull's-eye! You'll hit your *target* every time!

Life is much the same way. We'll always arrive at some destination or target, whether we aim or not.

However, if we focus our aim with a specific goal in mind, we might miss more often, but we'll significantly increase our chances of hitting something we intended to hit.

Like shooting arrows, when you set goals, you are essentially organizing a plan to hit a specific target. The goal becomes an objective or mission statement to help focus your attention and channel your effort.

Achieving a goal you have set, however, depends on your level of commitment, dedication, and concentration. Vague or hazy goals produce murky results. When you have difficulty setting and reaching your goals, you have not taken the time to visualize them in detail.

Keep in mind that some of your goals may be more important than others, or they may all be equally important so that you will need to prioritize them. To sort out goals, classify them according to three categories: short, medium, and long range.

Short-range goals are accomplished on a daily basis or within the next several months. Deadlines are essential.

Medium-range goals fall between one and several years. Both short- and medium-range goals should be very specific.

Long-range goals provide overall guidance and direction and don't need to be as specific. An example of a long-range goal would be, "When I retire, I want to live near the mountains with my family." Medium- and long-range goals are sustained and realized through the application of short-range goals.

It's time to have some fun and set a new goal for yourself. And by the way, there is no reason to wait for a New Year's Eve party to think about setting new resolutions for your future.

So, why not get a head start?

Be creative.

Use a colorful pen to write down your goal.

Then without delay, take careful aim at your *target*.

Now, fire your best shot without changing or moving the target.

Bull's-eye!

*It's not surprising how we can aim at nothing
and hit our target every time.*

How Were They Able to Do It?

They are able
because they think they are able.

— Virgil

A Big Lesson from Tiny Fleas

It's not that we have much in common with fleas, but a lesson can be learned from behavioral changes that fleas display upon graduating from the *flea training* academy. This academy consists of paper cups with formfitting lids, open-minded fleas, and a serious trainer bent on exploring the fascinating world of these bugs.

The fleas begin their training when the trainer places them inside a paper cup with its lid securely fastened to its brim. Initially, the fleas jump as high and as far as they can to catapult themselves over the top of the cup.

As time passes, however, they begin to realize the foolishness and futility of slamming themselves against the lid of the cup. As the fleas begin to accept their fate, the flea trainer prepares for their graduation.

It's at this point that the trainer removes the lid from the paper cup. Some of the fleas still jump, but not nearly high enough to reach the cup's rim. Amazingly, most just sit comfortably at the bottom of the cup.

People learn similar lessons.

Perhaps, early in life, they experienced something that kept them from stretching, reaching, or *jumping* to new heights. Just like the fleas, they too learned to stop trying because, even though a barrier or obstacle no longer existed, they believed the barrier was still in place, so they stopped trying.

It's a small thing, but next time you *jump*, go a little higher than you think you can or should.

You'll be amazed to discover that, just as with the flea academy, the *lid* was taken off of your life long ago.

A Fine Line Between Success and Happiness

Success is getting what you want–
happiness is wanting what you get.

— Charles F. Kettering

The Nest of Little Golden Eggs

In a distant land and time, the Greek writer Aesop wrote simple fables that are still read 2,500 years later.

One of his fables begins with a farmer who becomes fascinated with a goose that began laying beautiful golden-yellow eggs. Each morning the farmer would return to the goose's nest only to find another egg, equally as beautiful as the one before. To his surprise, however, the eggs were not like any he had ever seen before—they were solid gold!

Each day thereafter, the farmer anxiously returned to the nest to collect the next golden egg. With each passing day the farmer began to slowly acquire his wealth. Soon, however, his need for more eggs and riches overwhelmed his impatience with the goose that could lay only one egg each morning.

His mind began racing.

He knew what had to be done.

Wanting all the gold at once meant he would butcher the goose to collect all her eggs once and for all.

After the gruesome job was completed, a sense of shock and bewilderment fell upon the farmer's face. As he impatiently searched inside the goose for more golden eggs, he finally realized that no eggs were ever to be found in the nest again.

How many times have you felt like the impatient farmer—wanting everything at once?

Too often?

A simple lesson is learned from Aesop's fable.

Be patient.

Anything worth having is worth the wait.

Forecast Your Destiny

What you see as being possible,
what you believe as being likely,
and what you value as being sacred,
will be who you become.

— Raymond V. Haring

Enormous Success from Simple Values

Personal values are like traffic lights.
Without them—there's nothing but chaos.
With them—anything is possible.

Values are principles or qualities that each of us hold in high regard and find intrinsically desirable.

Consider the values of a man who was once told by a publisher that he had little or no artistic talent, who then decided to ignore the comment by imagining and building the most beautiful amusement park in the world with unparalleled service for its visitors. The amusement park is Disneyland and the founder was Walt Disney.

The success of the Walt Disney Company has been and continues today to be driven by simple principles that include dazzling entertainment and courteous customer service for all visitors.

Service or courtesy, like any other value, must be supported with absolute conviction.

Yet a value unsupported by actions is much like a table without legs. There is nothing to stand on.

Thinking about a value is actually much different than *living* it.

If you are unsure about your values, all you need to do is look at what you're doing, because it's your actions that reflect your values.

"What you value," writes Joel Weldon, "is what you think about. What you think about is what you become." Simple values have far-reaching consequences.

Value health—and you will become healthy.
Value strength—and you will become strong.
Value patience—and you will learn tolerance.
Value life—and you will live.
Value yourself—and you will have it all.

Change Your View—Change Your Life

Cherish your visions and your dreams,
as they are the children of your soul,
the blueprints of your ultimate achievements.

 — Napoleon Hill

See with Your Eyes—Navigate with Your Mind

There are as many different ways to see the world as there are ways to confront and solve the problems found in it.

One of the most powerful viewing techniques is visualization. We *see* things with our eyes, but we *view* or understand things with our mind.

Visualization, or *viewing*, is a process of imagining what has happened or could happen. People have been doing it for years, perhaps without knowing its immeasurable influence on their lives. Thoughts, memories, daydreams, fantasies, impressions, and dreams are examples of the visualization process. As a powerful vehicle for change, visualization can help us reduce stress, overcome fears, and achieve goals.

Visualization, however, can have two sides: one positive and the other negative. People who suffer from anxiety, worry, fear, and stress have mastered the unfavorable side of visualization. They see things that cause distress. Ulcer patients are *grand masters* at visualizing things that cause anxiety and worry.

Other people who apply the positive side of visualization create life's marvels of health, happiness, and peace of mind. They see themselves as visionaries who believe nothing is impossible. As dreamers, they have the freedom to shape their own lives and quite possibly, the lives of others.

Put your viewing power to good use.

Use your eyes to see and your mind to navigate.

Powerful Things Are Weightless

How much does a single thought weigh? This may seem like a silly question, but think about it—nothing is more influential or powerful than a single uninterrupted thought. Yet, despite their immeasurable influence, thoughts are intangible. They have no form or weight except as they exist in our minds.

Former U.S. Justice Oliver Wendell Holmes observed, "A moment's insight is sometimes worth a life's experience."

A single thought, lasting perhaps only a few seconds or moments, can be so powerful that it can make the difference between destroying a life or bringing about enormous pleasure, happiness, and success.

Every discovery or accomplishment throughout history, whether too small to be remembered or too important to be forgotten, can find its origin in a single thought.

Betty Nesmith's life was changed by a simple idea. Her idea appeared small when compared to other great accomplishments to which we can assign famous names. In the early 1950s, she noticed that the increased speed of electric typewriters resulted in more clerical typing errors. Putting two and two together, she mixed water-based paint with a coloring agent the color of clean white paper—and Wite-Out® was born.

Stories such as this teach us that even the smallest thoughts or ideas can have huge consequences.

You're Always Right

The mere idea that you *think* you can change is one of the most powerful thoughts you can entertain.

Holding a thought for a few seconds requires little effort, yet the prospect of change carries tremendous potential for freedom from self-imposed restraints and limitations.

Change can take as long as a lifetime, or it can take place in a moment. It begins when we act on a decision to do something differently.

All of us have the power to change if we believe we can. If we believe we can't, we won't.

Regardless of your choice, you're always right.

If you think you can,
or if you think you can't,
you are right.

— Henry Ford

Why Didn't I See It When I Saw It?

Have you ever walked in a field, only to return with literally hundreds of burr-like stickers stuck all over your socks and pants?

I have.

The experience left me not only irritated, but also thinking about throwing my socks away. After I pulled the stickers from my socks, I could see no advantage to dwelling on the matter, so my thoughts shifted to something else. It never occurred to me that a fortune could be made by giving thought to the little hooks on the small burrs that stuck two objects together.

George de Mestral, however, made the association. He saw the possible uses of manufacturing tiny burrs by seeing the same thing I saw, but from a different perspective. His annoyance with burrs led to the invention of Velcro.®

"Discovery consists of looking at the same thing as everyone else," according to famed scientist Albert Szent-Gyorgyi, "and thinking something different."

By viewing things from different angles, our perception and perspective of things change dramatically.

Consider, for example, the beauty, brilliance, and value of a diamond ring. Without light striking its surface, we could not differentiate between the most precious diamond in the world and a piece of broken glass. Simply allowing light to strike the surface of a diamond produces millions of vibrant colors.

Like burrs or diamonds, all things will appear differently based on how we choose to view them.

A Copper Penny Has More than Two Sides

We're only given two choices when we flip a coin, right? Heads or tails.

Ask anyone how many sides there are to a coin and they will probably say "two."

But all coins have three sides—the heads, the tails, and the rim!

Surprised?

Opportunities and answers to simple questions can be easily missed when we consider only the most obvious answer to a question. Often a mere pause or an extra moment of reflection will provide a different, and hopefully, more accurate, response.

There's a famous question that illustrates how opportunities are either created or lost based on what is seen or read into a question: Is there an opportunity to sell *new* and *improved* sunglasses to a group of people who have never seen or worn a pair of sunglasses? One person might conclude there is no interest or opportunity to market sunglasses to these people because they have never seen or worn sunglasses. This person's conclusion is based on the assumption that if these people had any interest in sunglasses, they would already be wearing them.

Another person, with more vision and imagination, might see the market as an untapped source of business because no one yet owns a pair of sunglasses.

Vision is one of the best ways to see things that others miss. Scientist and visionary Albert Einstein wrote, "Imagination is more important than knowledge."

Imagination, like vision, can be a tour guide helping us gain new insights that offer better answers to simple questions.

A Glimpse into the Future

Imagination is the preview of life's coming attractions.

— Larry Eisenberg

Little Details We Tend to Forget

I'll never forget meeting Buz Aldrin.
 Since then, every time I look at the moon, I'm reminded of my conversation with one of the first men to ever walk upon the surface of the moon.

Aldrin and other famous people have etched vivid images and memories deep inside our consciousness. Their accomplishments have truly transformed them into icons and living legends.

What do you think their lives were like before they reached *stardom* status?

Sometimes we think, "Oh, they were born a star," or "Their success was handed to them on a silver platter."

I believe any success, however defined, is earned one step at a time. Joe Girard once said, "The elevator to success is out of order. You'll have to use the stairs one step at a time."

Most of us instantly recognize the name Clark Gable, but not all of us remember or appreciate that he was not always a legendary actor. Before he became a movie star, he had a much different life off screen. Part of Gable's life was spent as a store clerk, mechanic, and lumberjack. It seems difficult to imagine that these times became part of his formative years. Each new job, each small step, and each new adventure or thought slowly moved Gable from an unknown clerk to a person immortalized on movie screens around the world.

The small steps each of us take may not seem to mark progress in any grand way and will most likely be easily forgotten. Still, each day is built with details that shape our destiny, and perhaps the destiny of others.

Few ever focus on the thousands of times Olympic gymnast Nadia Comaniche fumbled and fell during practice sessions. What history does remember about Nadia is her stunning performance that captured not only an Olympic gold medal, but the hearts and minds of millions who watched.

With each small step that you take in your own life, with each choice and decision that you make, you are literally building, shaping, and forming your life one step at a time. It's these individual steps that, when combined, help define who you are today and the person you will become tomorrow.

Believing that you have control over these individual steps makes it easier to recognize that you have the power to shape your own destiny.

So, approach your future one step at a time, one foot in front of the other.

Follow Your Thoughts

Our achievements of today are but the sum total of our thoughts of yesterday. You are today where the thoughts of yesterday have brought you and will be tomorrow where the thoughts of today take you.

— Blaise Pascal

Inspiration from Desperation

Need and struggle are what excite and inspire us.

— William James

Rejected All the Way to the Top

Quite frankly, I would rather be paid a compliment than dealt a rejection.

For most folks, compliments warm the heart and soul more than a brush-off or criticism. The concept of rejection, however, shouldn't dampen your spirit or lead you to question your resolve or commitment. Instead, you should view rejection as a means to sharpen your focus, hone your skills, and move you forward.

My attitude began to change when I stopped viewing rejections as personal insults or signals to abandon my goals and dreams.

Rejection is nothing more than a difference of opinion. If we can accept that a difference of opinion is okay, then we can begin to view rejection more objectively.

Frank Clark offers encouragement to anyone who views rejection as an obstacle: "If you find a path with no obstacles, it probably doesn't lead anywhere."

History is filled with stories of people who became famous by viewing rejection and obstacles as nothing more than guideposts that steered them toward their goals.

I can think of no man or woman throughout history who was rejected more often, who failed more often, and who was defeated more often before he reached his goal than the man who became the 16th president of the United States. His name was Abraham Lincoln. The unusual number of losses, rejections, failures, and defeats experienced by President Lincoln help explain his remarkable accomplishments and ascent to the top.

As long as we continue to strive, failures are inevitable. But if we don't try, failure is certain.

Thomas Watson, the founder of IBM®, had a very simple

formula for success, and one that is easily remembered: "The way to accelerate your success is to double your failure rate."

The next time you feel rejected or unsuccessful, just look back a step and you'll notice you're really two steps further ahead.

Enjoy your journey to the top!

An Inch to Go

If you're going to miss something, would you rather miss it by an inch or by a mile?

Some people would say that it doesn't matter because "a miss is a miss." It does matter, however, because most of us wouldn't allow ourselves to fall short of crossing the finish line if we knew we had only an inch to go.

Thomas Edison shed some light on this when he said, "Many of life's failures are people who did not realize how close they were to success when they gave up."

Ross Perot, a self-made billionaire, said, "Most people give up when they're about to achieve success; they give up at the last minute of the game, one foot from the winning touchdown."

Why do we give up so close to our goal?

One reason may be because we often overestimate how far we have yet to go and conclude we don't have the stamina to continue.

Because we cannot see around corners, it is difficult to estimate the distance between two points or the length between the beginning and the end of a goal. In fact, isn't it true that the last mile always seems the longest? This happens because we tend to concentrate on where we've been, rather than on where we're going.

Focus your thoughts on results and the finish line will appear closer.

If nothing seems to bring the finish line closer, then consider these thoughts by Jacob A. Riis: "When nothing seems to help, I go and look at a stonecutter hammering away at his rock, perhaps a hundred times without as much as a crack showing on it. Yet, at the hundred and first blow, it will split in two, and I know it was not that blow that did it, but all that had gone before."

One Good Obstacle Deserves Another

O bstacles are like weights. The more we lift or push them aside, the stronger we become.

The principle is simple. Resistance strengthens muscles and hardens bones. Obstacles challenge the mind and enrich the soul.

Repetition, coupled with resistance, builds not only strength, but endurance as well. The mind is no different than the body in this regard. You might initially feel a little tired from working your brain *muscles,* but as with an exercised body, you'll soon see and feel the difference.

In some respects, you could say we're much like trees.

J. Willard Marriott, whose name is recognized worldwide on the face of Marriott Hotels, knew this when he said, "Good lumber does not grow with ease; the stronger the wind, the stronger the trees."

Develop your *muscles*!

Clear the obstacles out of your way.

Taking Chances

You will never stub your toe standing still. The faster you go, the more chance there is of stubbing your toe, but the more chance you have of getting somewhere.

— Charles F. Kettering

One Step at a Time

It's easy to find excuses.

It's difficult, however, to find a way to make them work on your behalf.

No doubt, at some point in your life you were able to find more excuses to refrain from doing something than reasons for doing it.

It was John F. Kennedy who said that there are always risks and costs to a program of action, but they are far less than the long-range risks and costs of comfortable inaction.

The key to finding—or better yet, achieving—any form of success is to realize that big things cannot happen without consistently taking tiny action steps day after day.

I'm often encouraged by the story of a young man, uncertain of the direction of his life at the time he was working as a lifeguard at a swimming pool during the Great Depression. This man, knowing that he wanted to do more than teach children to swim, searched his heart and decided to take the steps necessary to pursue a career as a radio announcer. After failing many times to get any offers, he continued his search until one day he was offered a job as a sports announcer in a small town in the Midwest. These steps, like other small and courageous steps, ultimately led Ronald Reagan to become the 40th president of the United States.

Whether we're looking for a new career or a place in history, we can get there only by believing that we can, and then by taking steps that support our beliefs.

"The only thing that stands between a man and what he wants from life," wrote Richard De Vos, "is often merely the will to try it and the faith to believe that it is possible."

Be Like a Stamp!

What can a postage stamp tell us about determination and success?

Hidden on the back of each and every postage stamp is a very important message. In fact, the message is found in the glue itself.

Notwithstanding the value of the stamp, it's the stamp's ability to stick to an envelope that determines whether or not the mail is delivered.

Josh Billings made a powerful point when he said, "Be like a postage stamp. Stick to something until you get there."

A hundred dollar stamp won't get a ten cent letter to its destination if the stamp doesn't stick.

Simple, but true.

The probability of success increases tremendously when we adhere to a plan or goal until the job is completed or the goal is met. Incidentally, the failure rate approaches 100 percent when we abandon our plans.

So, be like a stamp. Stick to it.

It Could All Change in a Moment

A moment's insight is sometimes worth a life's experience.

— Oliver Wendell Holmes

A Moment of Time

*C*arpe diem.
Seize the day.
Life is short.

What great advice and wisdom do these philosophies offer? In a nutshell—learn from the past, anticipate the future, but *live* in the present.

The past is gone, the future hasn't yet arrived, so all we have is this very moment. Regardless of how long we exist, we live each day one moment at a time.

We decide how much of our own life is filled with special moments. Spending precious time trying to alter the past or hurry into the future will only steal time to explore and enjoy each day as it comes.

This book celebrates moments and how the smallest things can make the biggest differences in how we feel, think, and act. Simple thoughts and small steps taken now will pave roads to fulfillment and happiness.

Think positively and you'll feel positive. Think negatively and see how much harder it is to even crack a smile.

At any moment, we can quickly change how we feel by shifting our thoughts to uplifting images. Hans Selye, M.D., summed it up when he said, "Nothing erases unpleasant thoughts more effectively than concentration on pleasant ones."

Simple, but so essential to a life where the smallest things can have the greatest impact.

Keeping a Little Perspective

Have you ever lost your perspective?
Some folks have lost their perspective over things as trivial as dust balls, smudges, and scratches. To them, any scratched furniture or blemished floors would distract from fully enjoying precious moments in their *dream* home. Others have lost their perspective, if even momentarily, over a breezy day, a barking dog, a crying child, or any interruption they found too annoying or disruptive to handle.

Losing all perspective can lead to episodes of *tunnel vision,* which is a point of view so restrictive that virtually one idea or objective occupies your thoughts for excessive periods of time. It's analogous to dwelling on one topic or idea to the point of obsession, illness, or feeling an urge to escape.

A *one-track* mind misses so much, it's like walking through an art museum while looking down at your feet. Life passes us by and obsessions can become magnified and blown out of perspective.

Putting an end to tunnel vision begins with an awareness of new possibilities. New possibilities emerge when we simply shift our line of sight from the ground toward the horizon.

Oh—no!
It's much larger and more threatening than I first imagined.

Own Your Own Thoughts

*See things as you would have them be
instead of as they are.*

— Robert Collier

A Small Difference Makes a Big Difference

Could small adjustments in your attitude cause big changes in your life?

Absolutely!

"The greatest discovery of my generation," according to Harvard psychologist William James, "is that human beings can alter their lives by altering their attitudes of mind."

I couldn't agree more.

Our attitudes are greatly influenced by our belief system. Incidentally, these beliefs are learned from and shaped by our previous experiences.

As kids.

And as adults.

Personal judgments are made on the perception of these experiences. It's the evaluation of these experiences that produces the strong feelings or emotions we feel. After an emotion is sparked ... our attitude emerges.

As you can see, attitudes don't just happen. They unfold and mature with each new personal experience.

Just as attitudes are learned, they can be unlearned. This is great news for anyone who would like to have more control over their life. It all begins with improving our attitude about ourselves.

Consider the thoughts of insurance mogul Clement Stone. "There is little difference in people, but that little difference makes a big difference. The little difference is attitude. The big difference is whether it is positive or negative."

So, stay positive—make a big difference.

You're Always in the Driver's Seat

Take charge of your thoughts.
You can do what you will with them.

— Plato

Days in Our Lives that Never Happened

Now and then, most of us love to be scared. In fact, we'll even pay to be frightened.

To this day, Alfred Hitchcock's thrillers still do a pretty good job of scaring us. Certainly, there is no shortage of low-budget horror movies or paperbacks written with a slant to unsettle our nerves.

Still, there are even other ways to be terrorized.

Some people *scare* themselves by simply worrying throughout the day. People with insatiable appetites for terror, worry, or unrest typically indulge their subconsciousness with unpleasant dreams or early morning nightmares.

Mark Twain had keen insight into the minds of people who spend either too much time worrying about the future and past, or too much time dreaming up imaginary problems with terrifying consequences. He reminds us of the unnecessary misery caused by worry: "I have lived through some pretty terrible things—some of which actually happened."

Fear and worry are frightening emotions that can paralyze or cripple us from taking action in our lives. Both can be evoked by the anticipation of pain, danger, loss, or change—whether real or imagined. Fear and worry are based on two things: the uncertainty associated with change and a lack of confidence in dealing with unfamiliar circumstances.

Fear and worry also have no boundaries.

But there is hope.

To free ourselves from their grip, we must challenge fear and worry head-on, and be willing to step outside our *comfort spheres*, where things seldom change or improve.

In the most difficult times, when we're feeling the most insecure and vulnerable, the biggest and most rewarding changes can take place. By confronting fear, we refuse to be blinded by its facade.

When we run toward fear, it becomes exciting, but when we run from it, fear becomes debilitating.

Here's a simple solution to overcoming *fear*.

Face it.

Begin walking toward it.

And when you get near it—run as fast as you can through it! It feels much like running through a water sprinkler—exciting, but short lived!

You'll wonder why you didn't do it sooner.

Blinded by Sight

Stop it!
Stop it!
Stop it!
When you worry, you can't think.
When you don't think, you worry.

Are you starting to see the vicious cycle? Unfortunately, there's a very fine line between thinking and worrying. To notice the difference, you'll need to be on your toes.

Keep your balance!

"Worry is a thin stream of fear trickling through the mind. If encouraged it cuts a channel into which all other thoughts are drained," writes Arthur S. Roche.

Worry is nothing more than having an exaggerated concern with impending or imaginary situations.

When you worry, you're focusing thoughts on things that appear threatening, whether real or imagined. This may be the one time to keep your imagination in check.

Worrying also produces no results and offers no solutions to problems or challenges. If you spend more time working on solutions and less time worrying about problems, then there won't be any reason or time to worry.

There will only be time to think and act!

As a rule, men worry more about what they can't see than about what they can.

— Julius Caesar

Removing Doubts Removes Limits

Have you ever doubted yourself?
Do you want to know how to get around it?
The answer is simple.
Build confidence in your abilities.

Confidence erodes doubt. With fewer doubts comes freedom from nagging insecurities and self-imposed limitations.

If this idea sounds simple, then it can work for you. We build confidence by doing something over and over until we master it.

Walt Disney reminds us that we must believe whole heartedly in ourselves, leaving absolutely no room to question our abilities.

"Somehow I can't believe," Walt Disney wrote, "that there are any heights that can't be scaled by a man who knows the secret of making dreams come true. This special secret, it seems to me, can be summarized in four C's. They are curiosity, confidence, courage, and constancy, and the greatest of these is confidence. When you believe in a thing, believe in it all the way, implicitly and unquestionably."

Have the courage to believe that limits to your abilities do not exist.

With a little practice, your confidence will soar!

I Want Another Chance

As a boy, I remember anxiously waiting for the circus to roar into town. Watching the big silver trucks and trailers unloading outside the auditorium, I knew the circus animals were nearby.

On opening day, clutching a small bag of peanuts, I watched the clowns ride around on miniaturized fire trucks. They were amusing, but my thoughts and attention always returned to the animals—especially the trained elephants.

Elephants, like other powerful animals in the circus, are taught early to surrender their power, but not their strength.

While young, impressionable, and eager to learn, they are chained to immovable stakes driven deep into the ground. The heavy chains and steel stakes pin the young elephants in place. Eventually, they come to accept that any stake or leash, regardless of its size or strength, will bind and hold them permanently in place.

After countless tugs to free themselves from the stakes prove futile, the young elephants etch a lesson deep in the center of their brains. This lesson remains in place even as the elephants grow strong enough to pull free; unfortunately, they just *know* they don't have the will or strength to do so.

If the elephants would have given themselves another chance to exercise their will and strength, they would have been able to move just about anything, including the big silver trucks that brought them to the circus.

Imagine what is possible if you decide "I can," instead of thinking "I can't."

Need a Little Motivation?

Motivation is a *push* and *pull* phenomenon. All of us are pushed or nudged by inherent desires and needs— food, health, love, and security being our most basic needs. By the same token, we're pulled along by rewards and incentives— money and success being powerful motivators.

We can be driven to want something, but without an incentive, motivation eventually fades.

Have you ever found yourself in need of a little tug or nudge? Do you want to know where *motivation* comes from to change certain behaviors?

The answer is right in front of your eyes!

It's found in our *need* to avoid pain and seek pleasure and rewards.

Every End Has a Beginning

There is a universal law that is common to all undertakings: for every end, there must first be a beginning.

Consider the Nike® slogan, "Just Do It®."

Well, "Just Begin It" has plenty of merit, too.

Michelangelo's breathtaking frescos on the ceiling of the Sistine Chapel would never have been completed had Michelangelo not started at the beginning—by painting that first brush stroke on the ceiling.

Just starting, however, can be the most difficult thing to do. There is little doubt that the more things we begin, the greater the chance of seeing more things develop in our lives.

An end always has a beginning—just as a beginning has an end.

Reflect on the thoughts of novelist and philosopher Wolfgang von Goethe. "Are you in earnest? Seize this very minute. What you can do, or dream you can, begin it, boldness has genius, power, and magic in it. Only engage, and then the mind grows heated—begin it, and the work will be completed."

It makes no difference whether it's a step, a brush stroke, or a telephone call—begin it, and you'll make it happen.

No One Can Steer Parked Cars

The simplest rule in mathematics states that the shortest distance between two points is always a straight line.

Getting from one point to another, however, is slightly more involved.

There are three simple rules that explain how we maneuver from point A to point B.

Movement.

Movement.

And more movement!

The fastest sports car in the world that sits parked in a garage is no faster than an old rusty truck that won't start.

"Vision without action is merely a dream. Action without vision just passes time. Vision with action," Joel Barker wrote, "can change the world."

So, grab your keys and a map. Back yourself out of your *garage*.

It's time for the ride of your life!

Give Yourself Permission

It has been said that there are three kinds of people: people who make things happen, people who watch things happen, and people who wonder, what happened.

There's at least one more group to add to this list: people who wait for things to happen.

At one time or another each of us has fit into all four categories. But we've likely learned that personal fulfillment is usually achieved when we're one of those people who make things happen.

There will soon be more than six billion people on Earth. Only one of them is uniquely qualified to hand out *permission* slips to make things happen in your life the way you want them to happen.

You!

Too often, many of us get stuck hoping someone else will give us the nod or go-ahead to get started.

Giving yourself permission to take action is the first and biggest step you can take to move your life forward with purpose and accomplishment.

So put an end to waiting.

Give yourself permission to make new things happen in your life today!

Why Not?

Some men see things as they are and say "Why?"
I dream things that never were and say "Why not?"

— George Bernard Shaw

The Wishing Well

Inside each of us is a *wishing well* fed by a spring of consciousness called optimism. This well is actually a place in our minds where we give hope a chance to succeed. It's truly a wonderful place to collect our thoughts and reaffirm our faith that things will work out for the best.

But spending too much time simply wishing at this well can be counterproductive. Wishing can consume huge amounts of valuable time, leaving us with insufficient time to actually act on our wishes and make them come true.

It's time to visit the *wishing well*!

Make a wish.

After you make your wish, step away from the *well*. Now, begin focusing your thoughts, not on your wish, but rather on the tiniest steps you can take toward making that wish a reality.

All Great Things Had a Starting Point

Have you ever thought about starting a business or developing an exciting new product?

"Every vital organization," wrote James B. Conant, "owes its birth and life to an exciting and daring idea."

Regardless of the size of an existing organization or its strength as a company, at one time the business was no larger than the size of a single brain cell. That's right—every business, every product, every building, every flashlight, staple, or piece of tape, was once nothing more than an idea in someone's mind.

Because we're so accustomed to seeing the finished product in stores, we don't stop to think about all of the thoughts and steps that went into developing the product.

Millions of new businesses, products, and services are being developed every day. Remember, a new product or service doesn't have to be a totally new innovation. Much of what is *new* is just an improvement on old ideas or concepts.

It has been reported that Q-tips® were the creation of a man who noticed that his wife was cleaning the ears of their baby with little balls of cotton on small wooden toothpicks. A single thought led him to realize that it would be a terrific idea to attach little balls of cotton to the end of small sticks. The beginning of this multimillion-dollar product had, like all other new products, a starting point.

Any starting point is nothing more than a very simple imaginative idea begging to be born.

In Napoleon Hill's words: "Just as the oak tree develops from the germ that lies in the acorn and the bird develops from the germ that lies asleep in the egg, so will your material achievements grow out of the organized plans that you create in your imagination. First, comes the thought; then organization of that thought into ideas and plans; the transformation of those plans into reality. The beginning, as you will observe, is in your imagination."

Life's Highway!

No U-Turns on Bumpy Roads

When the going gets tough, are you one of the tough who get going? Or are you more prone to abandon a situation that suddenly turns difficult?

Are you disappointed when you stop short of reaching a goal? If so, rest assured, this is a normal response to anyone faced with challenges, bumpy roads, or rough seas.

Renowned inventor Charles F. Kettering said, "No one would ever have crossed the ocean if he could have gotten off the ship in a storm."

Would there have been a Ford automobile if Henry Ford had given up when faced with the many bumpy roads on which he rode? Henry Ford experienced huge financial setbacks several times before he began to see any success with his Model T.

Albert Einstein hit a huge roadblock when his Ph.D. dissertation was rejected by a committee at the University of Bern. Yet this devastating rejection by his colleagues did little to slow his flow of brilliant thoughts and contributions to the world.

Ludwig van Beethoven also avoided making U-turns. Deafness did little to derail Beethoven's talent and desire to write notes that would be translated into some of the most beautiful music ever heard.

Ask yourself what it is within you that keeps you on *bumpy roads* when you feel like turning around and heading back home?

Is it commitment?

Ambition?

Vision?

Once you determine what it takes to keep you from making U-turns on bumpy roads, you'll be miles ahead.

Easy Does It

There is no such thing as a big job.
Any job, regardless of size,
can be broken down into small jobs
which, when done, complete the larger job.

— Walter P. Chrysler

Don't Give Up on Your Last Attempt

One of the hardest questions to answer is, "When should I give up?"

The answer is—*after* you have achieved your goals!

Someone once said, "A man can fail many times, but he isn't a failure until he gives up."

One of the shortest and most famous speeches in history carried a similar message eloquently delivered by Sir Winston Churchill. "Never give up," he announced.

These three words are the foundation for success.

Perseverance, however, doesn't mean continually pursuing a dead-end path, beating dead horses, or repeating things that haven't worked.

Perseverance means working smart and with the notion that you will take the "one more time" approach to cross the finish line.

Remember Dr. Seuss, the famous author of children's books? We know of his work because he understood the "one more time" principle very well. His first children's book was rejected by more than twenty publishers. Had Dr. Seuss quit and not contacted more publishers, the phenomenal success of selling millions of copies of his book might not have occurred and his efforts up to that point would have been considered a series of failures.

And what about a scientist working for the 3M® Company who remembered that a colleague of his had developed a glue that many people considered totally useless because of its poor adhesive properties? Art Fry thought differently. He saw a success in a *failed* product. This *failed* product came to be known as Post-It® notes, one of 3M® Company's most successful products. The ability to write notes on a small piece of paper, stick them wherever you want, and then easily remove them later, makes Post-It® notes a must-have in every office.

The next time you think about giving up on an idea or project, think about Dr. Seuss or Art Fry at 3M®. They persevered and turned small failures into big successes.

You can do the same thing by not failing on your last attempt.

One Thing at a Time

You cannot be anything
if you want to be everything.

— Solomon Schechter

Common sense tells us that some tasks are just easier to do than others.

I was very young when I learned how to tie my shoestrings. At first, this was a big challenge, but now I lace my shoes without giving it much thought.

Most of us would agree that tying our shoestrings is one of the easiest things we can do. But what if we complicate the process by trying to lace both shoes at the same time?
Give it your best shot!

If we can't tie two shoestrings at the same time, what makes us think we can do two things more complex than lacing a pair of shoes at the same time with any better results?

"We cannot do everything at once," said Calvin Coolidge, the 30th president of the United States, "but we can do something at once."

We can choose from many options, but the *something* we select must be *one* thing.

A similar insight by Henry Ford made him both successful and famous. His thoughts about scattering a person's efforts: "A weakness of all human beings is trying to do too many things at once. That scatters effort and destroys direction. It makes for haste, and haste makes for waste. Every now and then I wake up in the morning with a dozen things to do. I know I can't do them all at once."

Doing one thing at a time is not a handicap, it's a blessing in disguise. It's a fail-safe mechanism that forces us to concentrate on one thing at a time, so that at least one thing gets done with our full attention.

You Will Feel It—After You See It

When you discover your mission,
you will feel its demand.
It will fill you with enthusiasm
and a burning desire to get to work on it.

— Clement Stone

I Did It on Purpose

Each of our acts makes a statement as to our purpose.

— Leo Buscaglia

Avoid the Biggest Mistake

Whether mistakes are big or small, we tend to think of them as errors in judgment or performance. In the old days, mistakes were called blunders or foul-ups. Most of us have made plenty of them. But making mistakes can have a positive side; wise people realize that mistakes can also be opportunities for learning.

Most of us are taught to avoid mistakes as if they were not a natural part of life. Yet successful people have a history of making mistakes riddled with failures.

Benjamin Franklin conveyed a wise thought when he said, "The man who does things makes many mistakes, but he never makes the biggest mistake of all—doing nothing."

The key point to learn about making mistakes is to benefit from them!

Enjoy a few mistakes now and then—you'll be sure you're not making the biggest mistake of all—doing nothing.

It Happens One Step at a Time

Great things are not done by impulse,
but by a series of small things brought together.

— Vincent van Gogh

Prioritize Your Spending List

Time is the most valuable thing a man can spend.

— Theophrastus, 278 B.C.

So Much Can be Done in So Little Time

On the next page, there are 1,440 dots, each dot representing one minute of a single day.

Pick one minute and imagine what you might be able to accomplish in just 60 seconds.

Try stretching for an entire minute.

Go ahead.

Stretch your arms, legs, or back for 60 seconds. You'll still have 1,439 minutes left over to do other things today.

Try offering a compliment to someone or call an old friend you haven't spoken to in many years. Either way, you'll still have time left over for yourself.

Or perhaps you could find several minutes in a day and really make big things happen. Exercising just one hour a week, leaving 99.4 percent of the week for less active moments, is one of the best ways to enhance your energy, vitality, and sense of well-being.

Benjamin Franklin once said, "If we take care of the minutes, the years will take care of themselves."

Just one short minute may be enough time to accomplish so much. Whether you choose to spend it complimenting someone, giving a tiny word of encouragement to a friend, or simply stretching and practicing relaxation techniques, you'll begin to understand the power each moment holds in your life.

Go ahead.

Savor a moment you won't forget!

Finding a Spare Minute in a Day Is Easy

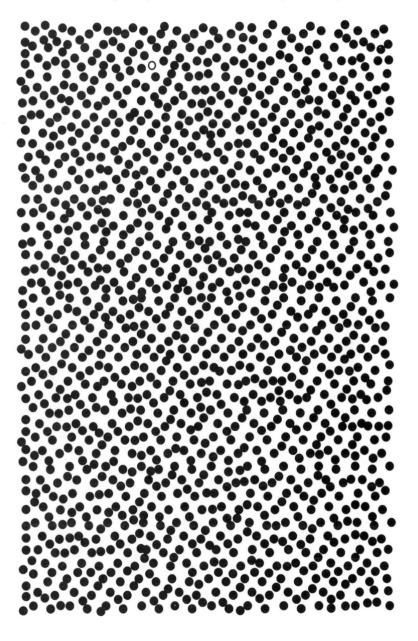

Now or Later

Those who think they have not time for exercise will sooner or later have to find time for illness.

— Edward Stanley, the 15th Earl of Derby

Someday

*S*omeday is a day sometime in the future that, for certain procrastinators, becomes the *eighth* day of a week or the best time to get things done.

This special day could be tomorrow or sometime much later. In any event, *Someday* exists for people who avoid doing things they believe they won't or can't do now.

When *Someday* does arrive, however, it's truly an amazing day. There's money in the bank and air in our tires. The weather is perfect. All the ducks, in all the ponds, all over the world, are all lined up in a row. Even the planets in our solar system are in alignment.

Will *Someday* ever arrive?

Yes, if *Someday* doesn't become the *eighth* day of the week or the *perfect* time to get things done!

Honey, let's start—
We don't get chances like this very often!

The Human Mirror

*The outer condition of a person's life
will always be found to reflect their inner beliefs.*

— James Allen

Searching for the Origin of Health

The Greek philosopher Socrates recognized that a person's susceptibility to disease and illness was linked to the quality of his or her thoughts when he wrote, "There is no illness of the body except for the mind."

Perhaps Socrates was a bit overzealous to suggest that all illness originates in the mind, but his observation of the existing link between mind and body is well understood today by virtually everyone in the medical community.

Just a few negative thoughts rehearsed in your mind can potentially make you feel physically ill. Since we have thousands of thoughts every day, the chances are great that a few negative thoughts will creep into our consciousness.

That's normal.

What is important, however, is how we handle or carry these thoughts and for how long.

All of us have mental tapes that we play in our minds. We have the ability to control how long, how loud, and how many times we play them. If a negative tape or thought pops in, pop it out! With a little practice it will be as easy as changing CDs in your CD player.

Begin by replacing one negative thought with one positive thought each day. Soon, you'll be amazed with the change in the tone and harmony of what you hear.

Post It on Your Refrigerator

L ooking to increase the performance of your refrigerator? Just stick an affirmation on it.

Affirmations are positive phrases, concepts, or images rehearsed over and over in your mind. Making affirmations is a way of gently preparing your mind to accept new ways of thinking.

Sending positive signals to your brain is a powerful technique for changing habits. There is nothing more inspiring and bolstering than affirmations that abound with optimism and enthusiasm.

Be honest: How often have you grown tired of pleasant thoughts, comforting suggestions, or a bandwagon full of cheering supporters?

I'll bet never!

Sometimes it takes only a glimmer of cheer or hope to change an attitude or perspective. That smidgen of faith may be found in as little as two words: I can. Or even one word: yes.

Affirmations are not cure-alls, but they do offer a way to send uplifting signals directly to your brain.

Go ahead, pick a message and send it special delivery. It won't cost you a dime.

Habits Wear Two Hats

S ome years ago, Orison Swett Marden said, "The beginning of a habit is like an invisible thread, but every time we repeat the act we strengthen the strand, add to it another filament, until it becomes a great cable and binds us irrevocably, thought and act."

Doing things over and over in a particular way forms strong habits. These habits can be big or small, productive or unproductive, healthy or unhealthy, wanted or unwanted.

Usually, we are not aware of the tremendous influence habits have on our character. Still, regardless of their nature, our habits become more entrenched as time passes.

John Dryden observed, "We first make our habits, and then our habits make us."

But just as they are learned, habits can be unlearned. Habits are managed by reinforcing healthy habits and weeding out those that are unhealthy or unproductive.

Unlearning begins with a single conscious thought that a particular action brings more pain than pleasure. Your thought must be followed by a decision to replace the old behavior with a new one.

Lasting change requires reinforcement, repetition, and time—much like the process that formed the initial habit.

Aristotle had the answer when he wrote, "Men acquire a particular quality by constantly acting in a particular way."

It's simple.

If you want to be a certain way—act a certain way.

Habit is either the best of servants
or the worst of masters.
— Nathaniel Emmons

Training Builds More than Muscles

There is nothing training cannot do. Nothing is above its reach. It can turn bad morals to good; it can destroy bad principles and recreate good ones; it can lift men to angelship.

— Mark Twain

Workout with a Friend

M eet one of the best friends you'll ever have to help burn fat 24 hours a day—whether you're awake or sleeping. Your muscles!

Strong, lean muscle tissue will always assist you in losing flabby pounds. If you aren't carrying extra pounds, then you can thank your muscles.

Here's how it works.

Muscle tissue thrives on burning energy—especially when we put our muscles to work. Unlike fat tissue, muscle burns tremendous amounts of energy, even when our muscles are resting. Fat tissue, on the other hand, thrives on storing energy.

Keep it simple.

Keep the muscle.

Lose the fat.

The more fat we wear, the more fat cells love to be fed because they have a ravenous appetite for maintaining their physique. A vicious cycle of weight gain may ensue if fat cells are allowed to call the shots. If we become inactive, our fat cells will work overtime to turn us into chubby balls.

In addition to exercising, the best way to keep your muscles from shrinking is to lose any unwanted weight very slowly.

Don't lose weight too quickly.

Losing weight too rapidly destroys valuable muscle tissue that acts as powerful fat burners. Focus on losing body fat, not on losing muscle and body tone. At this rate, you and your muscles will both be happy.

Hang on to your friends.

Give them what they need most—a regular workout.

Win More Often

Don't do anything in practice
that you wouldn't do in the game.

— George Halas

Fat Won't Burn Without Air

L et's talk about exercising. You may be surprised to learn that your body burns proportionately less fat as you increase the intensity of your workouts.

Biologically, it's impossible for muscles to burn fat unless they receive enough oxygen. Consequently, if your heart is racing and your lungs are rapidly expanding and contracting from fast breathing, your body is burning less fat.

The basic law that determines whether fat is being burned is quite simple. Fat, like fireplace logs, cannot be burned without oxygen present. If you have ever fanned a fire to get it started, you'll recognize that it's the same concept.

The next time you exercise with the intent to burn fat, keep the intensity down and the duration up. This minor adjustment will allow your heart and lungs to deliver the necessary oxygen to your muscles.

There are two basic types of exercise: aerobic and anaerobic exercise. Aerobic literally means "in the presence of oxygen." Muscles are at their best when they have plenty of oxygen. Anaerobic, on the other hand, refers to an activity where there is a shortage of oxygen.

We must continually breathe oxygen to live, regardless of the activities we do. In a sense, we're always doing aerobic activities—washing the car, taking a walk, working at the office, or reading this book.

Right?

Occasionally, however, we'll do something that gets our heart and breathing rate up. Perhaps a jog, a mountain climb, or a game of tennis is all it takes to elevate our heart and breathing rate. The activity remains aerobic if you're not straining for a breath of air. It's under these conditions that your body is *tuned* to burn fat for a longer period of time.

Activities become anaerobic when your body muscles are exercised so hard that the demand for oxygen makes it difficult to sustain the activity without gasping for air. The increase in heart rate and breathing rate is a gauge of how hard your muscles are working and how little fat you're burning.

Slow down.

Have some fun.

Burn some fat.

The next time you start to get out of breath, you'll know the real reason why you should slow your pace.

The Couch Potato Exercise Program

Think it's possible to be a *couch potato* 99% of the time and still greatly improve your health and physical shape by exercising just one percent of the time?

The dots below represent the number of hours in a week. (Yes, there are 168 hours in a week.)

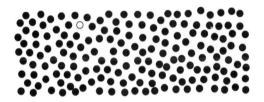

Doctors have known for years that the general health of the heart, and accompanying arteries that feed the heart, can be greatly improved by doing just three 20-minute aerobic workouts a week—graphically represented above by a clear white dot!

We don't have to climb to the top of Mount Everest to enjoy the benefits of a healthy heart.

If you're like most people, you don't like to exercise or can't find the time to exercise. If so, then consult the dot table again. It may help you realize that you still have 167 hours each week to recover from the weekly 60-minute *couch potato* exercise program!

Do the body good.

Stretch it.

Bend it.

Move it.

Be good to it.

In general, before starting any physical fitness program,
it's advisable to consult with your physician and get a physical
checkup if you are in doubt about your physical health.

100,000 Times a Day

If you have a healthy heart, most likely you don't think about it very often. But, there has never been a *pump* more amazing or forgiving than the human heart that thumps and pumps inside your chest. It beats miraculously 100,000 times a day, or about two and one-half billion times by the time you reach 65 years of age.

Each day we are given hundreds of chances to make healthy life-style decisions that will ultimately determine our final number of heartbeats.

Watching the things you eat, reducing the number of irritations and hassles, and moving your body more often are the simplest things you can do to bring peace of mind and health to your heart and body.

Right now, do one thing for your heart. List one artery-clogging snack or fatty food that you will stop eating today. Tomorrow, list just one activity or exercise that you will do once a day for a few weeks.

Your heart will thank you!

One Atom Makes a Big Difference

Meet Mr. and Mrs. Jones. They are so much alike, yet still worlds apart in many respects.

If you look at the illustration of the human male and female sex hormones below, you'll see that the tiniest difference in the chemical structure of these hormones is largely responsible for the difference between men and women. The secret is that Mrs. Jones' hormone has one more hydrogen atom than Mr. Jones' hormone.

Whenever I think about the smallest things that can make the biggest difference, I can't help but think about Mr. and Mrs. Jones and how one atom can have such a tremendous impact.

If just one atom can make such a big difference, think about the effect one positive or negative thought could have on how you feel at this moment.

Mr. Jones' Sex Hormone

Mrs. Jones' Sex Hormone

With a Single Breath

Puff!
Puff!
Puff!
Cough! Cough!

Did you know that the tobacco smoke emanating from both ends of a burning cigarette contains more than 4,000 chemical compounds?

Cough!

Incidentally, more than 40 of these chemicals are known cancer-causing agents.

The chemicals in tobacco smoke are *light* enough to linger in the air long after the smoker finishes his or her cigarette or leaves the room. Yet they're deadly enough to increase the risk of cancer, cardiovascular, and pulmonary diseases.

Sometimes, it's the tiniest chemical compounds that we can't touch, see, or feel that are the most harmful to the health of our lungs and bodies.

Cough!

Keep Your Protection Up to Date

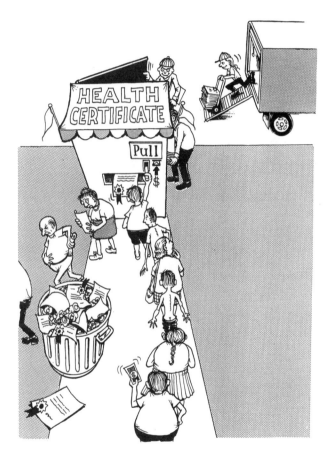

Hurry up with the paper!
Some folks are interested in buying some health protection.

It's the quality of our thoughts and actions, not certificates or *good* intentions, that determines our level of health. Keep your protection up to date—make healthy decisions.

Food for Thought

What you put in your brain is just as important as what you put in your mouth.

— Raymond V. Haring

I'm sorry, if he doesn't explode or say something soon—
I'm going to have to find something else to do.

Advantage for the Taking

Those who don't read books
have no advantage over those who can't read them.

— Mark Twain

The Biggest Nonfat Food Myth

L et's learn about food.
How many times have you stood at a grocery checkout stand only to be subjected to the many magazine covers featuring amazing new diets or miracle remedies for weight loss?

These magazines invariably feature pictures of slim women and men next to nonfat or low fat foods. When viewed together, this combination of images sets off a powerful subliminal association.

What a powerful message to convey to someone who likes to eat and yet would also like to be thin.

But, regardless of what you eat, if you eat it and don't need it, you will wear it. Don't misjudge this message—it's always a great idea to limit or restrict fat and calories to minimize the chance of gaining weight. But remember, any food we eat that we don't need will be metabolized by the liver into fat before being packaged, shipped, and hung on our bodies.

Many people fall prey to the illusion that they are eating fewer total calories a day when they consume diet foods or lower fat foods. They think, incorrectly, that they are on a diet because the food wrapper has the word *diet* on it.

In many cases this proclamation of fewer calories on the label is sufficient to tempt the dieter's interest for another helping or serving. In essence, they mistakenly assume that they are protected from weight gain by eating diet or nonfat foods that have fewer calories spoonful for spoonful.

It's really not a mystery.

People will just eat more low fat or nonfat foods. And as they eat more, they gain more weight—it just takes more time and more spoonfuls to get the job done.

People in our society are heavier today than ever before. Three out of four people in this country are overweight, despite the thousands of diet and low fat foods that they consume. And by the way, how many times have you seen a person eating a meat or cheese sandwich in one hand and holding a diet soda in the other hand, while they're watching a weekend of sports on television?

The concept is quite simple.

No one is dieting if they're eating a double western bacon cheeseburger with a 64-ounce diet soda and some nonfat potato chips.

You're dieting, however, when you make even the tiniest adjustments to your caloric intake. Eating just 100 fewer calories a day, the equivalent of eating one less slice of plain toast, may not seem like a significant change to your diet, but it's enough to cause your body to lose about 10 pounds of fat a year.

That's great news for not having to make huge life-style changes.

Remember, it's the *little* things that you eat or don't eat on a regular basis that makes the biggest difference in your weight.

Calories Don't Negotiate

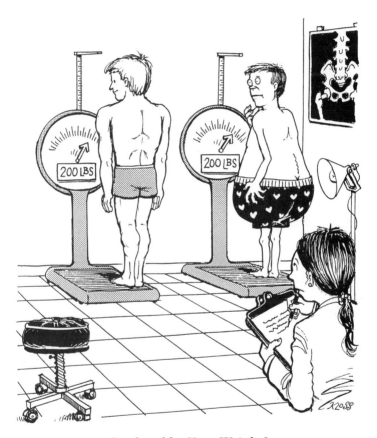

Confused by Your Weight?

L et's talk about inches and pounds. Weight control involves more than simply doing extra exercises and eating less food. The success of any diet ultimately hinges on unique circumstances.

First, consider your attitude about food. Are you over-eating because of loneliness, boredom, depression, or anxiety? If you're interested in losing weight, you might want to consider the following key points concerning dieting and weight loss.

Don't lose weight too quickly. Losing weight too rapidly destroys valuable muscle tissue that acts as powerful *fat burners.* Focus on losing body fat, not on losing muscle and body tone.

Muscle tissue is your best friend in losing flabby pounds. Muscle thrives on burning energy—especially when you put your muscles to work.

Unlike fat tissue, muscle burns tremendous amounts of energy, even when your muscles are resting.

Eat a high starch-based plant diet from different foods. This adds balance and variety to assure adequate intake of important essential nutrients. A high starch-based diet is low in fat and contains little or no cholesterol.

You may even get tired of eating.

You'll no longer be able to say, "I hardly eat and I gain weight."

You'll be eating all the time.

Eliminate fat from the diet wherever possible. Fatty sauces and toppings must be significantly reduced. Diets do not work if we eat fatty foods.

Fats are extremely high in calories.

If they're eaten, they'll live in little fat stores on your thighs, belly, waist, and chin.

Essentially, everywhere.

Avoid exotic diets. Shy away from diets made of expensive or unusual foods that are difficult to follow. Do you want to shop for these expensive or unusual foods for the rest of your life?

Foods should also be readily available and affordable.

Incidentally, there are no magical formulations or particular foods that will help the body burn fat faster.

Choose a diet plan for life. Who wants to lose weight only to gain it back?

No one!

There are two phases to weight loss.

Losing the weight.

And keeping it from returning.

Changing your diet and life-style will confront both issues. It would be wonderful to receive a stamped guarantee that keeps weight from returning. Unfortunately, no such certificate exists. Weight, health, and fitness are always subject to change.

Be patient.

It took time to gain weight, so it's going to take time to lose it. Avoid starvation or very-low-energy diets. Any diet will ultimately fail if it makes you feel hungry and weak.

Permanent weight loss involves life-style changes. Big dividends are ahead if you can modify your attitudes, habits, and beliefs about food.

Exercise! Start thinking about the shape and condition of your body and less about your weight.

The *weight* issue will take care of itself as you become more physically fit. Transferring the weight from the waist, chin, and buttocks to the biceps, shoulders, and back gives you a tapered, fit look and will burn any fat that is nearby.

Have fun.

Good luck.

So Small—Yet So Fattening

When it comes to alcohol, size doesn't matter. Although alcohol is chemically only one-sixth the size of common table sugar, it takes first prize for the *High-Energy Fuel Award.*

Jammed with calories, just one ounce of alcohol contains 210 calories, the equivalent of six teaspoons of lard! From a nutritionist's viewpoint, *alcohol* calories love to cling to our bodies.

Alcohol performs its dirty work by commanding the liver to make fat at a much faster rate than normal. When alcohol is broken down in the liver, powerful biochemical instructions are given to the liver to increase fat synthesis. The liver listens very carefully. Once fat is made in the liver, it is shipped out to be used or stored in adipose tissue.

Don't be fooled.

Even though alcohol may be as clear as water, it looks very different on our bodies.

Just an Extra Bite of Food

C oncerned about those pesky calories in the foods you love to eat?

There's good reason to be!

A calorie is a unit of energy so small that it takes about 3,500 calories to equal one pound of body fat. Often called a kilocalorie (kcal), the calorie is the easiest way for us to relate to the energy value of different foods and drinks.

Could a few extra calories a day be the reason why three out of four people in the United States are overweight or obese? Or is the mystery of weight gain hidden in the genes we inherit from our biological parents?

It is common knowledge that obesity runs in certain families. Special molecules in the nucleus of cells, called deoxyribonucleic acid or simply DNA, contain huge volumes of genetic information that allows physical traits to be passed on from one generation to another. All of us inherit certain genetic endowments that determine which biological instructions will be used to guide our physical development, from the color of our eyes to the size of our nose.

Inheriting a *bundle of traits* that instructs certain people to gain weight more easily than others is certainly another way genetic information makes its presence and influence noticed.

The real question is not whether genetics plays a role in obesity, but rather, to what extent?

Genetic instructions that alter a person's ability to burn calories by only **one percent** or approximately 20 calories (less than a mouthful of food) per day can lead to slow weight gain on the hips, butt, thighs, and stomach of many unsuspecting people. Biological factors, coupled with environmental factors such as nutrition, exercise, and life-style choices, work to determine exactly how much weight will be gained over time.

If you are *stuck* with fat genes, then overwhelm their influence with a little extra exercise. The 20 calories can be exercised away in many cases in about **one minute!**

Just think about the benefits if we routinely watched our diet and exercised at least five or ten minutes a day.

What if we all consumed a few more *fast foods* each day? Well, the results could be astounding!

Confused by the definition of fast foods?

Fast Foods are the Healthiest

L et's have a race! Who will get to eat first? The person who peels a banana? Or the person who drives through a drive-up fastfood window?

Foods that are baked, deep-fried, cooked, broiled, or processed require much more time to prepare than healthy *fast foods* that are simply handled or washed before they're eaten.

Still not convinced?

Consider the time difference between baking a cake or pie and making a fruit salad. You'll be finished eating your fruit salad long before the pie or cake is ready to serve.

If we slow down, reevaluate, and identify the *fast foods* we've been missing at the drive-up windows, we'll have more time to stock our kitchen with nutritious *fast foods*.

Good nutrition begins with eating nutritious foods to promote and sustain health.

We have a tendency to live longer when we eat to live, rather than live to eat.

The choices and decisions you make daily about what types of food to eat have a tremendous impact on your health and vitality. Food is much more than a source of energy; eating a variety of nutritious foods gives us the essential nutrients we need on a regular basis.

Essential nutrients must be obtained from our diet, since the body doesn't manufacture them. The six nutrient groups are carbohydrates (sugars and starches), lipids (fats), proteins, vitamins, minerals, and water.

Carbohydrate, fat, and protein are the three fuel nutrients burned by the body to provide energy. Alcohol is a rich source of energy, but it's considered a toxic nutrient and has no place among the essential nutrients.

Although we obtain zero energy from vitamins, minerals,

and water, certain vitamins and minerals act like spark plugs, setting energy-yielding nutrients on fire.

Vitamins and minerals do much more than burn fuels. As *organic* nutrients, vitamins are also required in very small quantities in the diet to perform many vital functions that include reproduction, vision, bone development, and blood formation and clotting.

Minerals are special types of *inorganic* nutrients that are also required in very small quantities for the purpose of serving the needs of billions of body cells. Some major functions include growth and repair of body tissues, transmission of nerve impulses, regulation of muscle contraction, maintenance of water balance, and structural roles.

Water is an important lubricant. It also works to cool and maintain normal cell operation.

Good nutrition leads to good living.

There's Only One Place You'll Find It

Have you ever felt a bit daunted by the thousands of diet and health books lining the shelves at bookstores with advice on how to improve your diet and reduce your intake of cholesterol—and maybe even the risk of heart disease?

Don't be confused or overwhelmed about cholesterol any longer.

From the seemingly endless combinations of foods that we consume, there are only two original sources from which all foods are derived: plants and animals.

There is, however, only one place to find cholesterol.

Animals.

The easiest thing to remember is that all plants, anywhere in the world, contain absolutely no cholesterol! You could therefore eat as many different kinds of fruits, vegetables, grains, cereals, nuts, and beans as you like and consume no cholesterol.

Incidentally, we have no need to consume any dietary source of cholesterol. All the cholesterol we need to make important compounds, such as vitamin D and male and female sex hormones, is made in the liver every day!

Remember, the small difference is in knowing which foods contain cholesterol. The big difference is the healthy payoff your body gets when you eat foods without cholesterol.

Sugar Can't Cause Cavities Without Permission

D id you know that sugar, by itself, doesn't cause cavities? It's the tiny organisms, known as bacteria, in your mouth that are responsible for dental decay. These bacteria need to eat just as we do.

After we eat, they eat.

Essentially everything we leave in our mouth after a meal becomes a banquet for bacteria. As they metabolize the *leftovers,* they produce organic acids that can lead to plaque buildup on your teeth. Their favorite meal to quickly increase their population is sticky sugar.

We can deny these scavengers their meals by removing their food supply by brushing and flossing. If you brush and floss, the army of bacteria in your mouth will die from starvation.

The secret to having healthy teeth is quite simple. It takes two ingredients to cause dental decay: food and bacteria. When one or the other is missing, your teeth are safe from attack.

Teeth are like people.

If they're ignored, they'll go away.

After Brushing—It's Time to Say Good Night

Finish every day and be done with it.
You have done what you could.
Some blunders and absurdities no doubt crept in;
forget them as soon as you can.
Tomorrow is a new day;
begin it well and serenely and with too high a spirit
to be cumbered with your old nonsense.
This day is all that is good and fair.
It is too dear, with its hopes and invitations,
to waste a moment on yesterdays.

— Ralph Waldo Emerson

Dream Under the Stars

Far away in the sunshine are my highest aspirations.
I may not reach them,
but I can look up and see their beauty,
believe in them, and try to follow where they lead.

— Louisa May Alcott

Keep Your Dreams Alive

How are dreams kept alive?

It's simple—by keeping your eyes on them, your muscles behind them, and your spirit in them.

Open your eyes.

Spread your wings.

Inhale deeply.

And dream big.

Remember, you can't *fly* if you allow your dreams to die.

Rise and Shine—the Morning News Is on Your Porch

"Tranquility Base" ... "The Eagles have landed."

"Roger, ah, some landings were a little softer than others."
"Ah" ... "Houston, ah, we'll keep you posted ..."

Houston—We Have a Solution

For some, it was Peter Pan. For others, the Wright brothers. And who still cannot marvel at the wonders of space travel? I've been fascinated with flying my entire life. My first experience with flying was making airplanes from school notepads. The paper airplanes were fun to toss, but I was always a little uneasy about where they would glide or land.

Still, my desire to fly progressed. Equipping myself with a pair of cardboard wings attached to my arms, I hurled myself from a small elevated launchpad in my backyard to the ground below. It was only after many disappointing trial jumps and skinned knees that I decided my career in the skies was finished. Many important lessons about my flying days, however, still surface from time to time.

It doesn't matter if I'm watching a sea gull embrace a coastal breeze or a telecast of a rocket launch from Kennedy Space Center in Florida, the message underscores the importance of *preflight* travel plans.

The idea of being able to take off from one destination and land precisely at another destination without getting off track would be more than a miracle if you didn't head *directly* toward your destination. In fact, it would be a miracle to come close to your intended destination if you're just one degree off when you leave your launch site.

For instance, if you were an astronaut traveling to the moon from Earth with a trajectory less than one degree off, your call back to Mission Control in Houston, Texas, wouldn't be "Houston—The Eagle has landed," but rather, "Houston—we have a problem—we're experiencing a flyby." You would miss your target by thousands of miles by being just one degree off!

Life, like traveling, is a journey. If our flight plan is even slightly off course, we, like birds, jets, and spacecraft, will fly right past our destination every single time.

This is a daunting thought, but there's good news.

As easy as it is to get off course, it's usually just as easy to get back on course. The key is to make any corrections toward your new direction as soon as possible. The sooner you make an adjustment in your direction, the smaller that adjustment will need to be.

In some instances, the difference between making and not making small adjustments can make the difference between success or failure, or perhaps between landing or crashing!

May I make a suggestion?

Aim for the stars.

Savor your journey.

Plan soft landings.

And enjoy your stay . . .

. . . wherever it may be.

From all of us at HealthSpan Communications, we hope you have enjoyed the thoughts and messages expressed in this book . . . and have in some special way been touched, inspired, and enlightened.

Coming soon, selections from this book will be narrated by the author, artfully orchestrated to beautiful music, and digitally mastered in CD and other audio formats.

New release by Raymond V. Haring, Ph.D.

ISBN   0-9643673-1-9 $14.95   264 pages

"A compelling analysis of myths and realities regarding alcohol. Good science. Good teaching. Read and learn. It will help you understand yourself, your family, and your friends. A thoughtful, concise explication of 176 topics related directly to alcohol, its use and abuse. Helpfully presented in alphabetical order."

George D. Lundberg, MD.
Editor-in-Chief, ***Journal of the American Medical Association***
American Medical Association, Chicago, Illinois

Notes

Notes

Notes

Notes

Notes

Notes